BREAKTHROUGH IS IN YOU

CONQUER 5 FEARS THAT KEEP YOU FROM ADVANCING

STUDY GUIDE

Copyright © 2021 by Jeff Scott Smith

Published by AVAIL

All rights reserved. No portion of this book may be reproduced, stored in a retrieval system, or transmitted in any form or by any means—electronic, mechanical, photocopy, recording, scanning, or other—except for brief quotations in critical reviews or articles, without prior written permission of the author.

Scripture quotations marked KJV are taken from the King James Version of the Bible. Public domain. | Scripture quotations marked NIV are taken from the Holy Bible, New International Version®, NIV®. Copyright © 1973, 1978, 1984, 2011 by Biblica, Inc.™ Used by permission of Zondervan. All rights reserved worldwide. www.zondervan.com. The "NIV" and "New International Version" are trademarks registered in the United States Patent and Trademark Office by Biblica, Inc.™ | Scripture quotations marked NKJV are taken from the New King James Version®. Copyright © 1982 by Thomas Nelson. Used by permission. All rights reserved. | Scripture quotations marked NLT are taken from the Holy Bible, New Living Translation, copyright © 1996, 2004, 2015 by Tyndale House Foundation. Used by permission of Tyndale House Publishers, Inc., Carol Stream, Illinois 60188. All rights reserved. For foreign and subsidiary rights, contact the author.

Cover design by: Joe De Leon
Cover photo by: Andrew van Tilborgh

ISBN: 978-1-954089-41-9   1 2 3 4 5 6 7 8 9 10

Printed in the United States of America

BREAKTHROUGH IS IN YOU

CONQUER 5 FEARS THAT KEEP YOU FROM ADVANCING

STUDY GUIDE

JEFF SCOTT SMITH

CONTENTS

PREFACE 6

Chapter 1. Breakthrough Is in You 10

Chapter 2. The Fear of the Unknown 18

Chapter 3. The Fear of Failure 26

Chapter 4. The Fear of Going First 34

Chapter 5. The Fear of Investment 42

Chapter 6. The Fear of Opposition 50

Chapter 7. Sustaining Breakthrough 58

PREFACE

*May our footprints not only take us to our destiny,
but may they also forge a trail for others to follow.*

As you read the "Preface" in *Breakthrough Is in You*, review, reflect on, and respond to the text by answering the following questions.

REVIEW, REFLECT, AND RESPOND:

What do you think inspired Jordan Romero to conquer Mt. Everest at only 13 years of age?

_____

_____

_____

_____

_____

_____

_____

How would you describe the common thread of "breakthrough" as exemplified in the lives of Romero, Neil Armstrong, Rosa Parks, and Roger Bannister?

_____

_____

_____

_____

_____

_____

_____

_____

What role does fear play in your life in terms of suppressing your desires or inhibiting your goals?

_____
_____
_____
_____
_____
_____

What are you prepared to commit to to overcome those fears and achieve breakthrough?

_____
_____
_____
_____
_____
_____

CHAPTER 1

BREAKTHROUGH IS IN YOU

When you have the dynamic of breakthrough working in your life, it gives you the calm, the confidence, and the courage to push back and break free. Be determined not to live your life in a box. Experience the freedom and liberty you were created to enjoy!

As you read Chapter 1: "Breakthrough Is in You" in *Breakthrough Is in You*, review, reflect on, and respond to the text by answering the following questions.

REVIEW, REFLECT, AND RESPOND:

When have you observed other people experience breakthrough? What did that look like?

_____
_____
_____
_____
_____
_____
_____
_____
_____

What instances in your life has fear threatened to steal your hopes and dreams? When has false evidence attempted to steal your authentic purpose?

_____
_____
_____
_____
_____
_____
_____
_____
_____

How do you think God wants to help you break free from the confines of your past or current fears?

_____
_____
_____
_____
_____
_____
_____

Why do you think breakthrough is such a difficult process?

_____
_____
_____
_____
_____
_____
_____

What resources do you possess—in your hands and in your head—to lead you towards breakthrough?

_____
_____
_____
_____
_____
_____
_____

How will boldness and courage help you when you feel like you are not making enough forward progress toward your goal?

_____
_____
_____
_____
_____
_____

What is your attitude toward living your life outside of the comfortable box you have always known? Traditionally how determined/stubborn have you been when it comes to expanding your boundaries?

_____
_____
_____
_____
_____
_____

Whom do you admire for his or her personal breakthrough? What is that person's story?

_____
_____
_____
_____
_____
_____

> *When the time came for her to give birth, there were twin boys in her womb. As she was giving birth, one of them put out his hand; so the midwife took a scarlet thread and tied it on his wrist, and said, "This one came out first." But when he drew back his hand, his brother came out, and she said, "So this is how you have broken out!" And he was named Perez. Then, his brother, who had the scarlet thread on his wrist, came out. And he was named Zerah.*
>
> —Genesis 38:27-30 (NKJV)

Consider Genesis 38:27-30, and answer the following questions:

What was so remarkable about this birth?

_____
_____
_____
_____
_____
_____
_____
_____
_____

What is the significance of the second child being born first?

_____
_____
_____
_____
_____
_____
_____
_____
_____

How does this story of breaking through apply to your life?

_____

_____

_____

_____

_____

If Zerah represents Christ, and Perez, a believer, what does it mean to you that Christ allows His believers to go before Him?

_____

_____

_____

_____

_____

CHAPTER 2

THE FEAR OF THE UNKNOWN

It is dangerous to become comfortable with one's current condition or position because there is much more available! If you believe that your current condition is normal, you will lack the tenacity, courage, fortitude, and boldness to change it. If you are convinced that where you are in life is the best that it will ever be, you will settle for that.

As you read Chapter 2: "The Fear of the Unknown" in *Breakthrough Is in You*, review, reflect on, and respond to the text by answering the following questions.

REVIEW, REFLECT, AND RESPOND:

What was so radical about JFK's challenge to make it to the moon?

_____
_____
_____
_____
_____
_____
_____
_____
_____

Reflect on Armstrong's iconic words, "One giant leap for mankind. . . ." What events have transpired in your life that have felt epic and monumental? If you can't think of any, try to identify why. Is it lack of opportunity or fear that has held you back?

_____
_____
_____
_____
_____
_____
_____
_____

What role has uncertainty played as you've made various decisions in your life?

_____
_____
_____
_____
_____

What does faith look like in your mind?

_____
_____
_____
_____
_____

What have you found helps you focus on or envision the potential good in outcomes rather than the negative?

_____
_____
_____
_____
_____

What experiences might interfere or hinder one's capacity to focus on the good?

_____
_____
_____
_____
_____

What is the difference between reaching for more in life and being ungrateful or discontent?

_____
_____
_____
_____
_____
_____

Consider the steps that breakthrough people take. How can you employ these step in your life?

_____
_____
_____
_____
_____
_____

What do you need to purposefully engage in that will push you beyond your zone of comfort?

_____
_____
_____
_____
_____
_____
_____

> *The Lord had said to Abram, "Go from your country, your people and your father's household to the land I will show you. I will make you into a great nation, and I will bless you; I will make your name great and you will be a blessing. I will bless those who bless you and whoever curses you I will curse; and all peoples on earth will be blessed through you." So Abram went, as the Lord had told him; and Lot went with him. Abram was seventy-five years old when he set out from Harran.*
>
> —Genesis 12:1-4 (NIV)

Consider Genesis 12:1-4, and answer the following questions:

What promises did God make to Abram?

_____
_____
_____
_____

What assurances did Abram have that God would come through on His word?

_____
_____
_____
_____

What consequences can you envision had Abram not been faithful? What kind of existence would the Hebrew nation have endured without its true "founding father?"

_____
_____
_____
_____

CHAPTER 3

THE FEAR OF FAILURE

Breakthrough people see failure as a teacher and not as a judge. They allow failure to teach them lessons but not to define their identity. Breakthrough people do not base their self-worth on their successes or failures. They live from the inside out. They do not allow their mistakes to determine who they are. They know that their worth is determined by who God has created them to be, not by what they do.

As you read Chapter 3: "The Fear of Failure" in *Breakthrough Is in You*, review, reflect on, and respond to the text by answering the following questions.

REVIEW, REFLECT, AND RESPOND:

Is your natural inclination to stick with what you know or venture into unknown arenas despite the risk of failure? What do you see as the strengths and weakness of each?

_____
_____
_____
_____
_____
_____
_____
_____
_____
_____

What is your takeaway from the rather humble origin story of Steve Jobs?

_____
_____
_____
_____
_____
_____
_____
_____

What is your experience with failure? How have you regarded it in terms of anticipating or planning for your future success?

_____
_____
_____
_____
_____
_____

If the measure of your life were to be based on your commitment to trying again and again, on a scale of 0 to 10—0 being never and 10 being always—how would you measure your life? Explain your rationale.

_____
_____
_____
_____
_____
_____

Consider the quotes from Thomas Edison regarding discouragement. When have you observed someone who was just inches from a goal, but gave up before he or she reached it? What can you learn from that person's experience?

_____
_____
_____
_____
_____
_____

> *For though the righteous fall seven times, they rise again, but the wicked stumble when calamity strikes.*
>
> —*Proverbs 24:16 (NIV)*

Consider Proverbs 24:16, and answer the following questions:

What wisdom do you see in this verse?

_____
_____
_____
_____
_____

Why do you think a man is considered righteous even if he continues to fall?

_____
_____
_____
_____
_____

How could you encourage someone who seems to continue making missteps or falling down?

_____
_____
_____
_____
_____
_____

How is *staying down* an expression of doubt in God?

_____
_____
_____
_____
_____
_____
_____
_____
_____

Of the five steps Jeff proposes to help you break the fear of failure, which one do you perceive to be your greatest challenge? How can you can overcome it?

_____
_____
_____
_____
_____
_____

How could your fear of failure be a way you are attempting to conceal certain inadequacies? What are these, and how can you begin to tackle them?

_____
_____
_____
_____
_____
_____

Imagine your worst-case scenario—losing your dreams, landing on your face, losing relationships, family, etc. What would recovery look like? Generate a timeline, then contemplate the reality of what failure and rebuilding would entail.

_____
_____
_____
_____
_____
_____

CHAPTER 4

THE FEAR OF GOING FIRST

There is a risk in not taking a risk! In failing to take a risk, you risk losing future success, achievement, and fulfillment. You forfeit your chance to make a difference and live out your purpose in your own life and in the lives of others. By counting the cost of missed opportunities, you will realize that you stand to gain so much more by taking the risk.

As you read Chapter 4: "The Fear of Going First" in Breakthrough Is in You, *review, reflect on, and respond to the text by answering the following questions.*

REVIEW, REFLECT, AND RESPOND:

Contemplate the gravity of James Meredith's actions and their implications. How did his bravery impact the country and the pages of history?

_____
_____
_____
_____
_____
_____
_____
_____
_____

The words of John F. Kennedy not only inspired a mission to the moon but James Meredith's decision to apply to college. Who provides such inspiration for you?

_____
_____
_____
_____
_____
_____

Consider this person and write down at least two things they have said that make you want to tackle your fear and dare to be the first.

_____
_____
_____
_____
_____
_____
_____

Meredith faced a wall of bureaucracy and laws that were constructed to prevent his success. Sometimes certain rules that are in place are antiquated and designed to perpetuate a system of injustice. How do you feel you are prepared to take on such rules should the occasion arise?

_____
_____
_____
_____
_____
_____

Overthinking led the golfer to make mistakes, lose his advantage, and with it, the Masters title. When have you allowed your mind to take over with thoughts that have derailed your success?

_____
_____
_____
_____
_____
_____

Jeff writes that even when you are essentially paving the way, doing something no one has done before, Christ has still gone before you. What are ways you can keep in mind this divine trail that has already been forged?

_____
_____
_____
_____
_____
_____

How can you implement Jeff's practical points of breaking the fear of going first into your life?

_____
_____
_____
_____
_____
_____

What talents, abilities, and resources do you already possess that qualify you to be a pioneer? How can you better access them and put them into action?

_____
_____
_____
_____
_____
_____

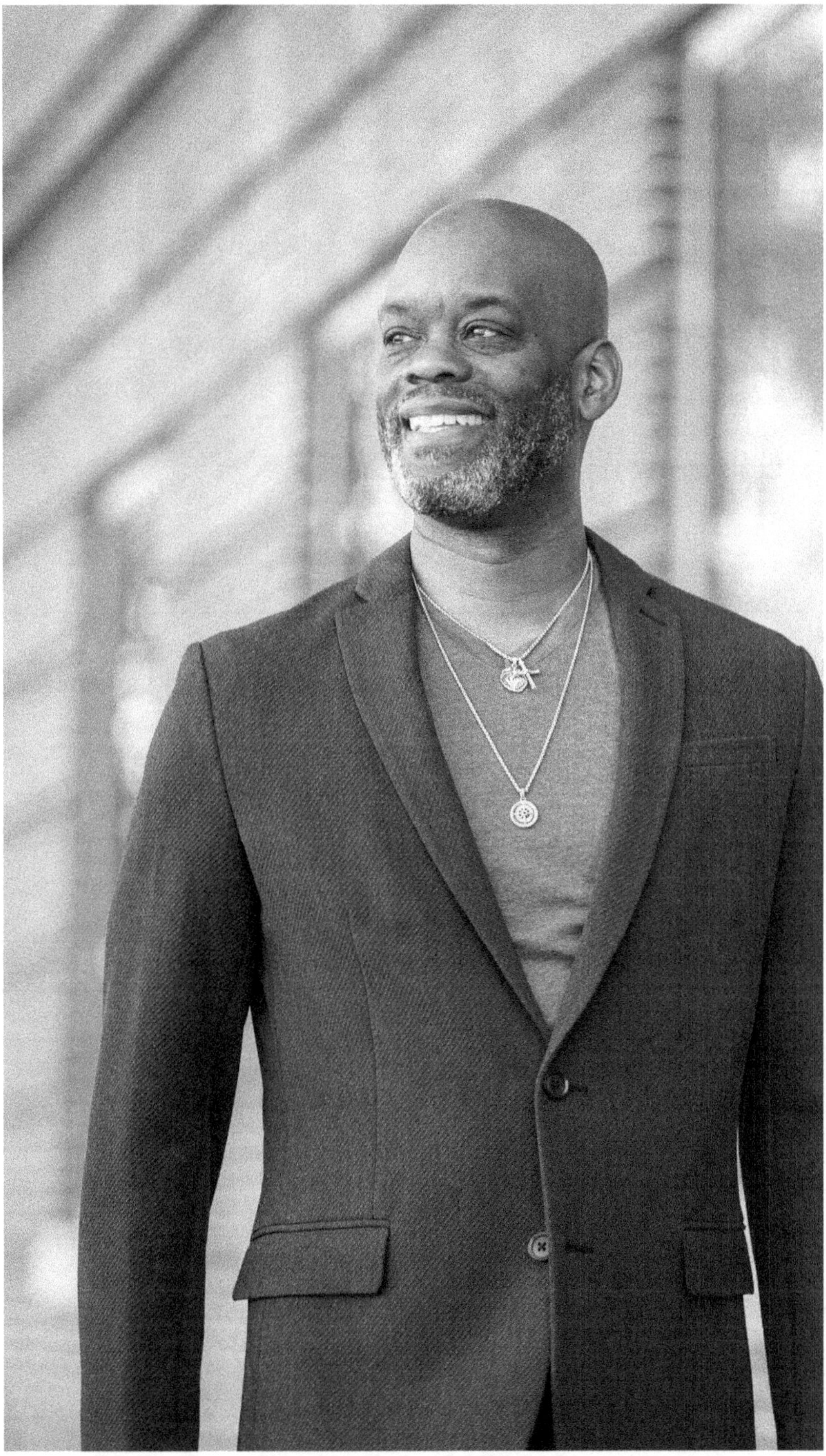

> *"Come," he said. Then Peter got down out of the boat, walked on the water and came toward Jesus.*
>
> *—Matthew 14:29 (NIV)*

Consider Matthew 14:29, and answer the following questions:

What was the scenario facing Peter as Jesus was calling to him?

_____
_____
_____
_____

What would have happened if Peter had given in to fear and never stepped out of the boat?

_____
_____
_____
_____
_____

Even though he eventually slipped below the surface, what can you learn from Peter's steps of faith?

_____
_____
_____
_____
_____

When has God called you to "walk on the water?" What was your response?

CHAPTER 5

THE FEAR OF INVESTMENT

Breakthrough leaders have a perception of work that is positive, not negative. Their approach to it is purposeful and intentional. They do not see it as something they have to do. They see it as a necessary tool for building their dreams.

As you read Chapter 5: "The Fear of Investment" in *Breakthrough Is in You*, review, reflect on, and respond to the text by answering the following questions.

REVIEW, REFLECT, AND RESPOND:

Whom do you admire who has invested wholly in his or her dreams and calling from God?

_____

_____

_____

_____

_____

Though she would eventually become world renowned, Teresa's initial investment into her call to ministry cast her into abject poverty. What was the return on her investment? How satisfied would you be with such a reward?

_____

_____

_____

_____

_____

_____

_____

_____

_____

What does it look like to invest yourself in your work and in the things in which you believe?

_____
_____
_____
_____
_____
_____
_____

How does work help us to hold on to the promises of God?

_____
_____
_____
_____
_____
_____
_____

Consider your personal fitness journey. Is it exemplary of a significant investment over time or is that an arena you wish to improve? What plans can you enact to do so?

_____
_____
_____
_____
_____
_____
_____

How does David demonstrate the practice of investment? What can you learn from his life?

_____
_____
_____
_____
_____
_____
_____
_____

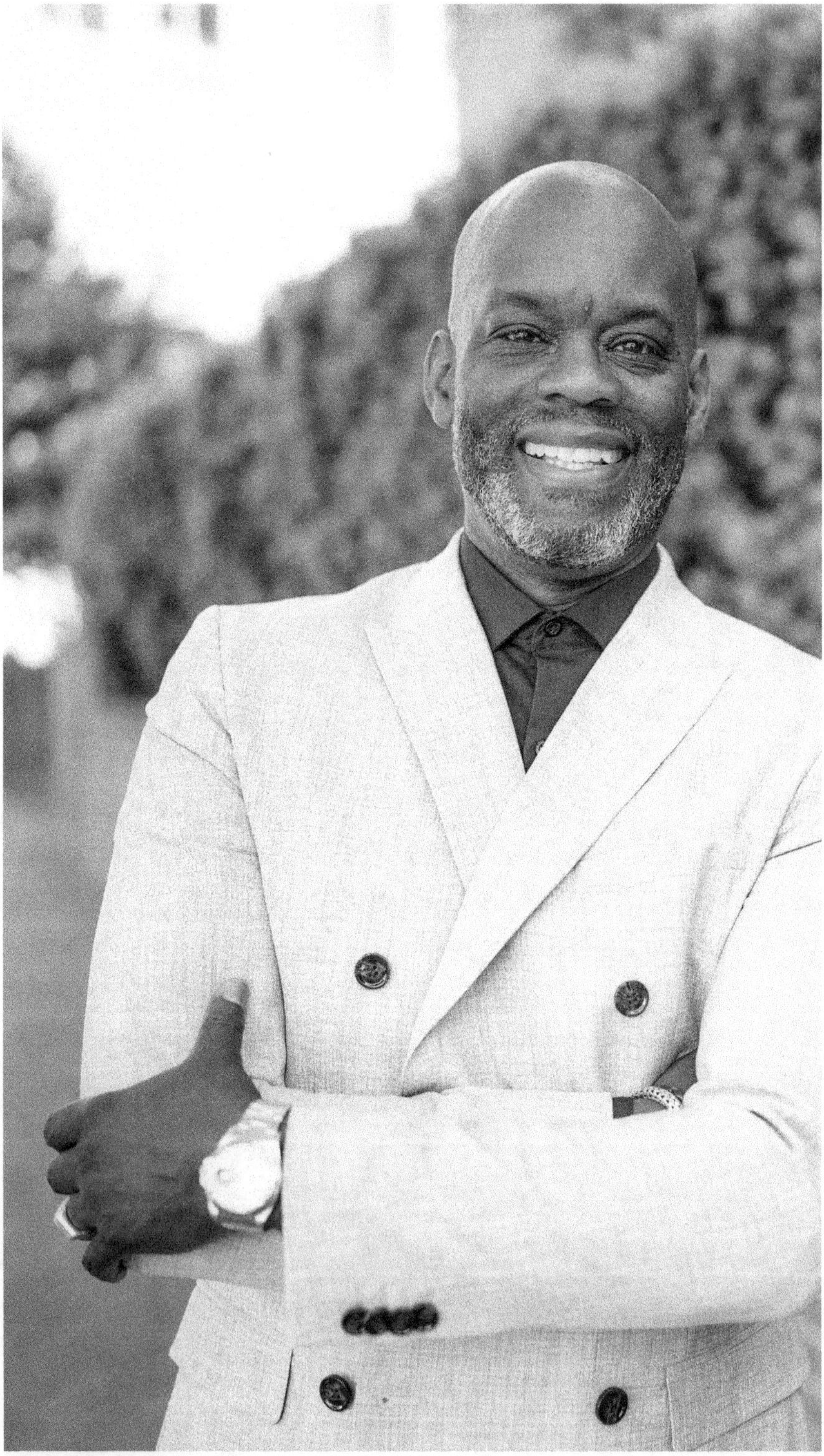

What distractions and powers do you expect to encounter that may threaten to steal, kill, and destroy your confidence, promise, or desire? What is your plan to overcome them?

_____

_____

_____

_____

_____

_____

_____

Is the pain of past defeats inhibiting your willingness to invest? How can you use what once hurt you to help you?

_____

_____

_____

_____

_____

_____

_____

How will you incorporate the three practical points Jeff lays out to overcome your fear of investment?

_____

_____

_____

_____

_____

_____

> *Those too lazy to plow in the right season will have no food at the harvest.*
>
> *Proverbs 20:4 (NLT)*

Consider Proverbs 20:4, and answer the following questions:

Why are we sometimes tempted to be lazy or not put in the work even when we know what the outcome will be?

_____
_____
_____
_____
_____

When have you observed someone else's inability or refusal to work come back to bite them? What can you learn from his or her unfortunate experience?

_____
_____
_____
_____
_____

In what ways can you motivate yourself when you feel like doing nothing?

_____
_____
_____
_____
_____

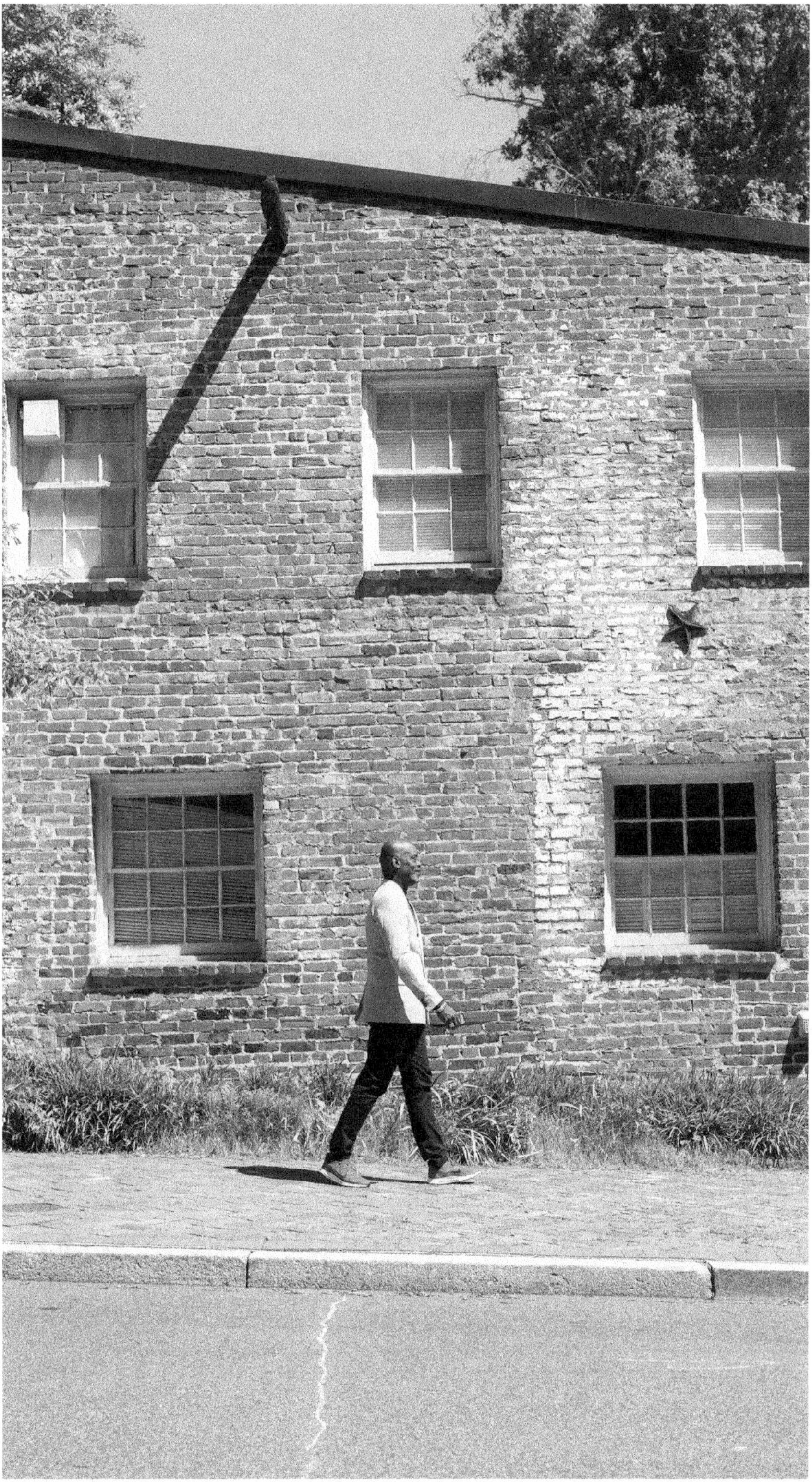

CHAPTER 6

THE FEAR OF OPPOSITION

When life kicks you, make it kick you forward. In life, adversity is inevitable. In any significant pursuit, there will be opposition. No one is exempt from it. Adversity comes to expose who you are on the inside. Ordinary people, many times, become bitter when faced with adversity. Breakthrough people, however, become better.

As you read Chapter 6: "The Fear of Opposition" in *Breakthrough Is in You*, review, reflect on, and respond to the text by answering the following questions.

REVIEW, REFLECT, AND RESPOND:

Nelson Mandela's life is a masterclass in overcoming opposition. What do you find particularly inspiring?

_____
_____
_____
_____
_____
_____
_____
_____

What is interesting about Mandela's reputation continuing to grow while he was in prison? What does this say to you about the strength of opposition and the power you have to thwart it?

_____
_____
_____
_____
_____
_____
_____
_____
_____

Jeff suggests that sometimes opposition may in fact be opportunity in disguise. Reflect on an instance when you encountered opposition. How can you reframe this resistance into something you could use to better your outcome? How might you apply that to current opposition?

_____
_____
_____
_____
_____
_____
_____

Do you live your life expecting rejection? When have you used this as an excuse to back away from your goal?

_____
_____
_____
_____
_____

How would your life change if you lived as if you believed there were a "yes" hanging over you all day long?

_____
_____
_____
_____
_____

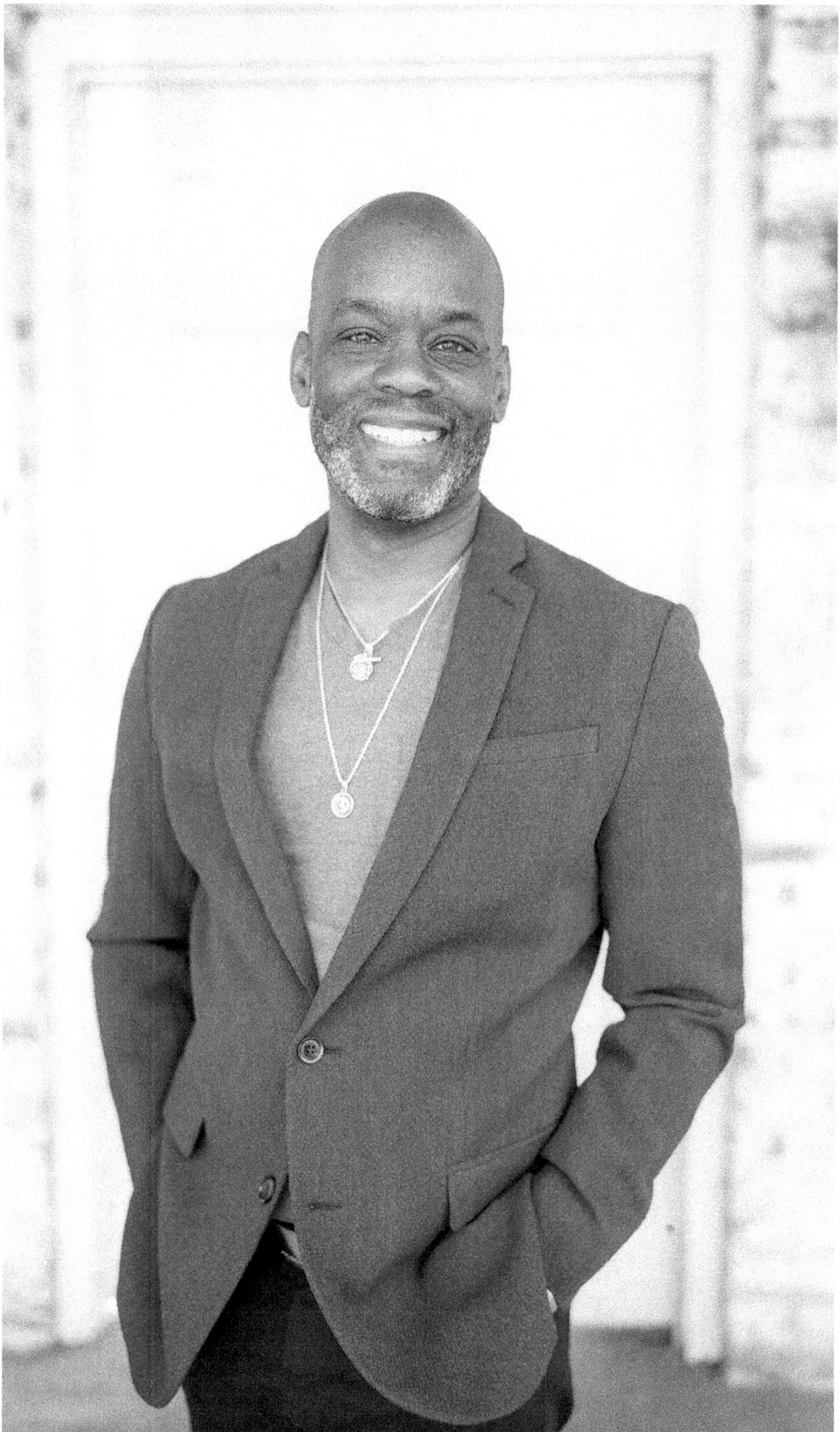

Picture Caleb and Joshua in the Promised Land. When have you seen the promises of God—the grapes and the milk and honey—but also the giants and obstacles of opposition? In which did you trust to prevail? Moving forward, how can you continually remind yourself that God's promises are infinitely more powerful than man's obstacles?

_____
_____
_____
_____
_____
_____

If you've ever thought that opposition meant that God was out to get you, what can you now see was the fallacy in that line of thinking? How can you retrain your thoughts to recognize God's leading even in the midst of opposition?

_____
_____
_____
_____
_____
_____

How can you implement Jeff's four points of practice in your life?

_____
_____
_____
_____
_____
_____

> *Greater is he that is in you, than he that is in the world.*
>
> —*1 John 4:4 (KJV)*

Consider 1 John 4:4, and answer the following questions:

Why might God offer you His reassurance that nothing in this world is beyond His power?

_____
_____
_____
_____
_____

How can His words help you when you are feeling overwhelmed by opposition?

_____
_____
_____
_____
_____

With the knowledge you have of the power of Christ, how might you encourage someone else who is discouraged?

_____
_____
_____
_____
_____

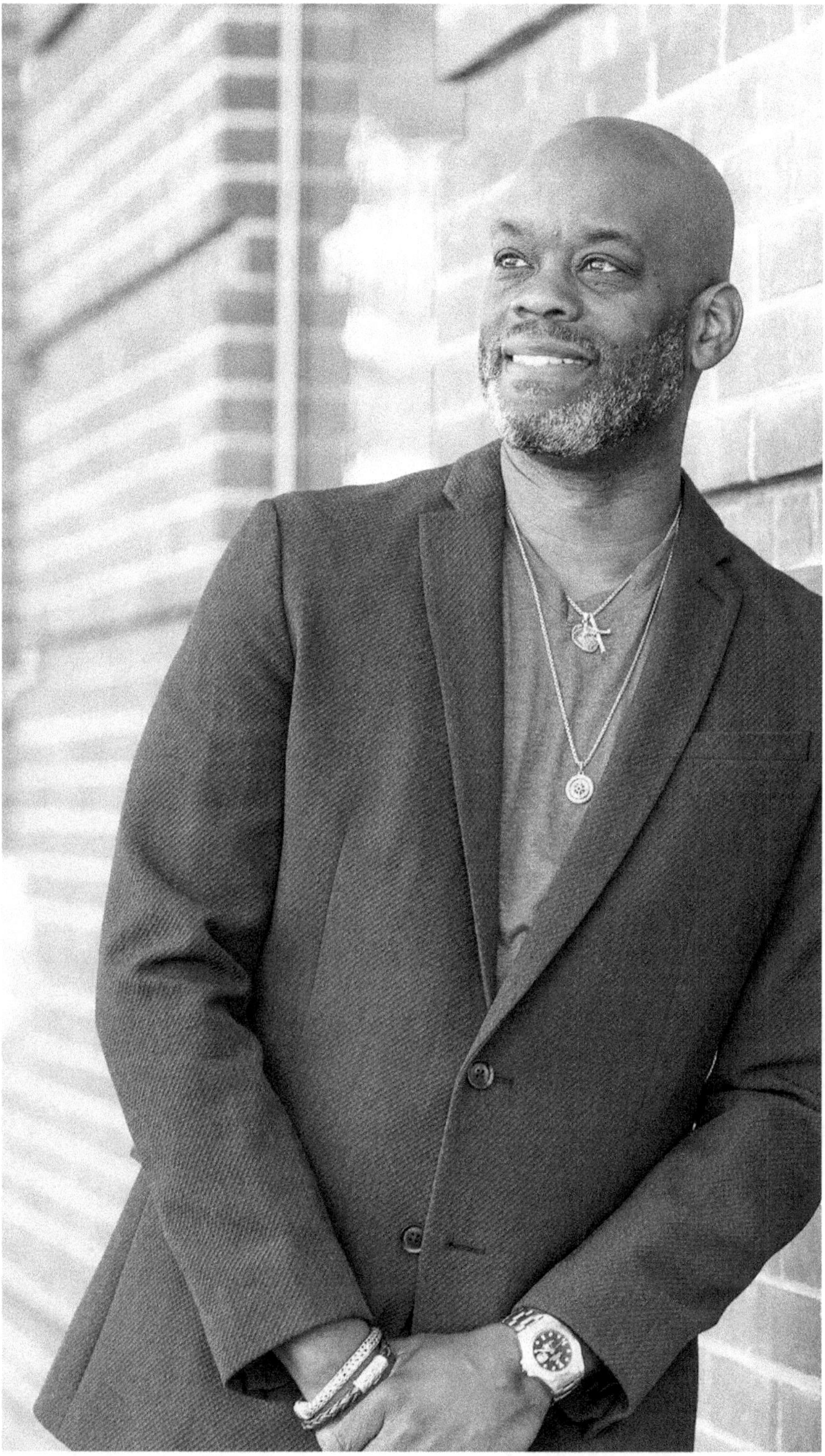

CHAPTER 7

SUSTAINING BREAKTHROUGH

How many ideas or plans have you had that remained simply ideas and plans? Where did they go wrong? Was it the idea? Was it the planning? Or was it that you never executed them?

As you read Chapter 7: "Sustaining Breakthrough" in *Breakthrough Is in You*, review, reflect on, and respond to the text by answering the following questions.

REVIEW, REFLECT, AND RESPOND:

What can you take from this book to strengthen your resolve to conquer your FEAR?

_____
_____
_____
_____
_____
_____
_____
_____

Of the five fears Jeff outlined, which is the most challenging for you personally? What is your plan to systematically and consistently counteract it?

_____
_____
_____
_____
_____
_____
_____
_____
_____
_____

Consider Neil Armstrong, Mother Teresa, and James Meredith. Whose story resonated most clearly with you? How can you carry the tenets of its teaching within you?

_____
_____
_____
_____
_____
_____

How does Jordan Romero's feat at Mount Everest make you reconsider the time you have spent and the time you have left to seize the moment?

_____
_____
_____
_____
_____
_____

> *Fear grows out of the things we think; it lives in our minds. Compassion grows out of the things we are and lives in our hearts.*
>
> —Barbara Garrison

Consider the quote from Barbara Garrison and answer the following questions:

How can you begin to shift your thinking to overcome your fear?

_____
_____
_____
_____
_____

Consider the life and death of Jesus. He lived knowing full well how He would die. Yet He lived a life of compassion, action, and boldness. How can you emulate His example to reach breakthrough in your life?

_____
_____
_____
_____
_____
_____

> You gain strength, courage, and confidence by every experience in which you really stop to look fear in the face. *You must do the thing which you think you cannot do.*
>
> —Eleanor Roosevelt

www.ingramcontent.com/pod-product-compliance
Lightning Source LLC
LaVergne TN
LVHW020112220825
819277LV00037B/654